Pine Road School Library
Huntingdon Valley, Pennsylvania

Given in Honor of
Zach Medina

December 2001

Wishing You a Very Merry Christmas
and a Happy New Year!

All Our Love,
Mom & Rick

Christmas
TREES

Christmas
TREES

Kathryn Stevens

THE CHILD'S WORLD, INC.

Library of Congress Cataloging-in-Publication Data
Stevens, Kathryn, 1954–
Christmas trees / by Kathryn Stevens.
p.   cm.
Summary: Describes the origin and significance
of using evergreen trees at Christmastime,
how they are grown, cut, and shipped, how
to choose a good tree, and how to care for it.
ISBN 1-56766-638-8 (lib. bdg. : alk. paper)
1. Christmas trees—Juvenile literature.
[1. Christmas trees.]   I. Title.
GT4989.S74   1999
394.2663—dc21   98-55730
                 CIP
                 AC

Photo Credits

© Comstock, Inc.: 30
© 1993 Dan Dempster/Dembinsky Photo Assoc. Inc.: 15
© 1994 Dan Dempster/Dembinsky Photo Assoc. Inc.: 9
© J. Faircloth/TRANSPARENCIES, Inc.: 26
© Kelly Culpepper/TRANSPARENCIES, Inc.: 2
© Les Saucier/TRANSPARENCIES, Inc.: 10
© 1998 Mark E. Gibson: 29
© Mauritius–H. Schwartz/Photri, Inc.: 24
© Randy Wells/Tony Stone Images: 13
© Sylvain Grandadam/Tony Stone Images: cover
© 1994 Terry Donnelly/Dembinsky Photo Assoc. Inc.: 19
© Tony Stone Images: 6
© Walt Anderson: 16, 20, 23

On the cover...

Front cover: This giant Christmas tree is standing at EuroDisney in France.
Page 2: This neighborhood in North Carolina has lots of Christmas trees.

Table of Contents

You are sitting in your cozy living room, sipping hot chocolate in front of a glowing fire. In the corner of the room stands a big green tree. It is covered with colorful decorations and lights that blink on and off. Piled around the tree are beautifully wrapped gifts. You watch the blinking lights and think how pretty the tree looks. It's your very own Christmas tree!

← This beautiful Christmas tree is decorated with lights and bows.

Why Do We Decorate Trees for Christmas?

Throughout history, people have made trees and branches a part of many holidays. In Germany and Scandinavia, people brought trees inside their homes during the long, snowy winter. The trees reminded them of the greenery and warmth of summer. In Germany, people started using decorated trees as part of their Christmas celebrations. The idea spread to other countries, including the United States.

During the 1800s, Christmas trees became very popular. Songs were even written about them! The Christmas carol "Oh, Tannenbaum" is all about Christmas trees. The word *tannenbaum* (TAN–nen–bowm) means "fir tree" in German.

This tree is decorated with old ornaments and toys. ⇒

What Kinds of Trees Make Good Christmas Trees?

What happens to elm and maple trees in the fall? Their leaves change color and fall right off. If you brought a maple tree inside, you would have nothing to decorate but a big stick! That is why Christmas trees are made from **evergreens**—trees that keep their green leaves all winter long. An evergreen's long, thin leaves are called **needles.**

⇐ It is easy to see the needles on this *pine* tree.

Many kinds of evergreens are used for Christmas trees. *Pines,* including *Scotch pines,* have long, soft needles that stay on the branches for a long time after the tree is cut. *Spruce trees,* such as *Norway spruce,* have short, stiff, sharp-ended needles that fall off more quickly.

The needles of *fir trees,* including *balsam fir,* are a little longer and flatter. They stay on fairly well, as long as the trees aren't cut too early. The *Douglas fir* isn't really part of the fir family, but it looks like a fir. It holds onto its flat, inch-long needles well and is a popular choice for Christmas.

These *spruce* branches have short needles. ⇒

What Are Artificial Trees?

Some people do not like to use real trees for Christmas. Instead, they use **artificial** trees—trees that are not real. Most artificial trees have wire and plastic branches covered with plastic needles. The branches connect to a tall, upright holder that takes the place of the tree's trunk.

Some artificial trees are hard to tell from the real thing unless you look very closely. Others are made to look quite different from real trees. Some are even bright pink or shiny silver! If they are packed and stored carefully, artificial trees can last for many years.

It is hard to tell whether this tree is real or artificial. ⇒

Evergreen trees grow wild in many regions of the country. Some people cut wild trees to use for Christmas. They must be sure to get permission from the person who owns the land! One problem with using wild trees is that they do not always grow in nice, Christmas-tree shapes. That is because they must compete with other trees for sunlight and room to grow. Instead of cutting wild trees, most people buy Christmas trees that are specially grown on tree farms. Many regions of the country have Christmas-tree farms.

⇐ These wild pines aren't keeping nice "Christmas tree" shapes.

How Are Christmas Trees Grown?

Growing nice Christmas trees takes several years and a great deal of care. First, baby trees called **seedlings** are planted in long, straight rows. As they grow bigger, the seedlings are thinned until they stand five or six feet apart. That gives them plenty of room to grow. When the trees are about two feet tall, the growers start clipping the tips of the branches to give the trees a nice shape. Clipping the branches is called **shearing.** The growers also watch for signs of diseases or pests.

These seedlings are growing on a farm in Washington state. ⇒

How Are Christmas Trees Cut and Shipped?

When a tree is big enough to make a good Christmas tree, it is marked for cutting. If it is not green enough, the growers spray it with tree-green coloring. The growers must cut the trees at the right time. They must cut the trees early enough to ship them to the sellers. But if they cut them too early, the trees will dry out and start to lose their needles. People are not happy if their Christmas tree loses its needles right away! Most Christmas trees are cut in late October or November.

⇐ These *Douglas firs* have been cut down and placed in a pile.

After the trees are cut, they are shaken to get rid of any dead, brown needles. Then they are wrapped in twine or plastic netting. Wrapping the trees is called **baling** them. Baled trees are easier to stack, store, and load without breaking any branches. Some large trucks can carry 1,000 baled trees! The trucks carry the trees to the places where they will be sold.

Sometimes trees are sold hundreds of miles from where they were grown. Cut-off branches are saved and sold, too. They are used for decorating and for making round Christmas **wreaths** that people hang on their doors.

These trees have been baled and are ready for market. ⇒

Can Christmas Trees Cause Problems?

As beautiful as they are, Christmas trees cause some problems. Long ago, people decorated Christmas trees with lighted candles. That was very dangerous, because the trees could catch fire! Electric lights have made decorating much safer, but Christmas trees must still be treated carefully. You should make sure your tree is away from heaters and fireplaces. Always turn off the tree's lights when you leave the house.

⇐ Like long ago, this tree is lit with candles instead of electric lights.

Christmas trees cause some environmental problems, too—especially after Christmas is over. Americans throw away millions and millions of trees every year. Disposing of so many trees is a problem! Many communities use large machines to grind the trees into small chips. Some people set their tree outside and use it as a bird feeder for the rest of the winter. Others use a living, potted Christmas tree that they can keep indoors or plant outside in the spring.

⇐ This tree has been placed on the curb for the garbage collector.

How Can You Choose a Nice Christmas Tree?

Choosing a tree can be lots of fun. First you need to decide how big a tree to get. Then you can think about what type to get. Should you get a tree with long needles? Short needles? Needles that will stay on for a long time? Whatever kind you decide on, make sure it is nice and fresh. The needles should be green and bendable and stay on the branch. If they are brown or brittle or fall off, the tree was cut too long ago. It's mostly a matter of finding the tree that's right for you!

This family is cutting down the large tree they have chosen. ⇒

How Should You Take Care of Your Tree?

Even though the tree is no longer growing, it still needs water. When the tree was cut down, the raw end sealed itself with dried sap. After you buy the tree, be sure to trim off the end. That creates a fresh surface that soaks up water. Put the tree in its stand right away, and make sure it never runs out of water. It's best to set the tree away from bright sunlight, radiators, or other heat sources, too. All those things will make it dry out faster and start losing its needles.

Now you've chosen your tree, brought it home, and found the perfect spot for it. It's covered with decorations and twinkling lights. It doesn't really matter whether the tree is real or artificial, tall or short, or long-needled or short-needled. All Christmas trees carry the same message: "Have a Merry Christmas!"

⇐ This beautiful tree is all decorated for Christmas.

Glossary

artificial (ar–tih–FIH–shull)
Something that is artificial is not real—even though it might look like the real thing. Artificial Christmas trees are made from plastic and metal.

baling (BAY–ling)
Wrapping cut trees in twine or netting is called baling them. Christmas trees are baled to make them easier to handle and stack.

evergreens (EH–ver–greenz)
Evergreens are trees with leaves that stay green all winter instead of changing color and falling off. Many kinds of evergreens are used for Christmas trees.

needles (NEE–dullz)
The thin, pointy leaves of an evergreen tree are called needles. Different kinds of evergreens have different kinds of needles.

shearing (SHEER—ing)
Shearing is cutting the ends of a tree's branches to give the tree a certain shape. Christmas-tree growers use clippers or knives to shear the trees into a pleasing shape.

seedlings (SEED–lingz)
Seedlings are very small trees. On Christmas-tree farms, evergreen seedlings are planted in long, straight rows.

wreaths (REETHZ)
Wreaths are round rings made of branches. Many people decorate their doors with Christmas wreaths.

Index